Australian LANDSCAPES

CONTENTS

A Land Apart

Australia, a land where vistas stretch from horizon to horizon, is composed of contrasts and extremes: sapphire-blue skies arch over shimmering desert plains; exquisitely coloured birds fly through towering rainforests; white surf pounds on golden sand; rain and floods are followed by drought and fire; and the wildlife is as unique and diverse as the land itself.

Everything about Australia is on a grand scale – beaches can run for over 100km, rivers for several thousand, outback properties are measured in millions of square kilometres and wheat fields stretch as far as the eye can see. With some of the oldest rocks and tallest trees in the world, it is a land that has been home to the Aborigines for over 40 000 years yet European settlement only occurred a little more than 200 years ago. Today, Australians are united in trying to protect and respect their magnificent land instead of attempting to dominate it.

Top: A cluster of granite boulders makes up the Devils Marbles in the Northern Territory.

Above: Tasmania's Gordon River glides through World Heritage-listed rainforest.

Opposite: Sunrise bathes the Murray River as it flows alongs its epic journey to the sea.

Right: Wheat fields shimmer in the summer heat on South Australia's fertile plains.

Below: Yellow Waters, Kakadu National Park, is renowned for its prolific birdlife.

Land of Extremes

Covering over 7 600 000km², Australia lies in the southern hemisphere between the Indian and Pacific oceans and stretches from the tropical waters of the Coral Sea in the north to the icy reaches of the Southern Ocean. Most of the population lives on the seaboard as both the east and west coasts of Australia enjoy a warm, temperate climate. The eastern seaboard in particular has rich, fertile soils and much of Australia's farming industry is based in the lush pastures found there.

In the hot and humid tropics of northern Queensland, the Top End and the Kimberley, vegetation flourishes, creating magnificent rainforests such as those of the Daintree in Queensland and the wondrous wetlands of Kakadu National Park. Each year the tropics experience the 'Big Wet' – the summer monsoon rains which start around October and last until the end of March.

By contrast, the arid centre is characterised by landscapes where temperatures fluctuate from 50°C at midday to 0°C at night. Vegetation changes from grasslands to scrub country before turning into the silent beauty of sandy desert. Dry forest, dominated by eucalypts, is most common in Australia, particularly around the coast. The narrow strip to the east of the Great Dividing Range also contains rainforest which is most dense in northern Queensland. The wet forests to the south-east of the country are less dense and contain the

beautiful mountain ash, one of Australia's tallest trees, and other hardwoods. Tasmania has ancient forests of Huon pine and Antarctic beech, while the karri forests of south-western Australia are equally spectacular.

Although much of Australia is arid, it is nevertheless crossed by many rivers. Some are relatively short, flowing from the ranges to the coast but inland there are mighty rivers like the Murray and the Darling which rise in the Eastern Highlands and flow westward towards South Australia, meandering across the continent for thousands of kilometres. They are the lifeblood of the drought-prone areas through which they pass; however, in periods of prolonged drought even these mighty rivers can cease to flow.

Australia is acclaimed the world over for its glorious beaches, coastlines, and island splendours. These range from the wild and rugged cliffs of the Great Australian Bight and Port Campbell National Park in the south to the vast unspoilt sandy beaches of Fraser Island and the tropical island paradises of the Whitsundays off the Queensland coast.

At the opposite end of the spectrum, snowscapes abound during the winter months in the alpine regions of the Snowy Mountains, the Victorian Alps and the highlands of Tasmania. There is a pure and breathtaking beauty in the sight of majestic eucalypts laden with snow under an arching blue sky. Above the tree line the forests give way to heath and in spring these alpine meadows are a mass of delicate wildflowers.

Above: *Winter snow enhances the pristine beauty of Tasmania's Cradle Mountain–Lake St Clair National Park.*

Bottom: *Surf rolls onto golden sands at Town Beach, Port Macquarie.*

Opposite bottom: *Carved by waves from the roaring Southern Ocean, the Natural Bridge is a spectacular feature of Torndirrup National Park, Western Australia.*

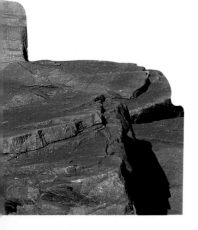

Below: *No one who sees Uluru glowing red under a violet sky could fail to be moved by this Northern Territory landmark.*

Left: *Jagged limestone columns emerge from a moonscape of wind-blown sand in the Pinnacles Desert, Western Australia.*

A Continent Sculpted by Time

The diversity of Australia's landscapes is the legacy of aeons of dramatic geological activity combined with more than 3000 million years of grinding and whittling by the elements. The west, for example, contains some of the oldest rocks in the world dating back to when the land was still part of the supercontinent of Gondwana: journeying through the magnificent region of the Kimberley is like travelling back in time.

Known as the island continent, Australia comprises two significant landmasses – the mainland and the island of Tasmania – and can generally be divided into three areas: the Eastern Highlands, the Central Lowlands and the Great Western Plateau. The Eastern Highlands are home to some of Australia's highest mountains – including Mount Kosciusko at 2230m – and extend from Cape York to Tasmania. The Central Lowlands run north to south through the centre of the continent and once formed the bed of a great inland sea, while the Great Western Plateau spreads from the Red Centre to the west coast.

To trace the story of Australia's landscapes, we have to journey back to between 110 and 45 million years ago – the time when Australia broke away from Antarctica and started to drift north, a process that continues at a rate of 1 to 2cm a year. Throughout this period the elements shaped and sculpted the natural wonders for which Australia is famous today: Uluru, the Great Barrier Reef and Tasmania's Cradle Mountain, among others.

Around 36 to 25 million years ago, volcanoes began erupting along the eastern seaboard from Queensland down to Victoria and into South Australia. Volcanic remnants can still be seen in Queensland's spectacular Glasshouse Mountains, the Warrumbungles of New South Wales, and Mount Gambier in South Australia. This volcanic activity, combined with the folding and faulting of the earth's crust, created the Great Dividing Range, a dramatic boundary between the tablelands in the west and the coastal ranges. It extends for over 3000km from Cape York in Queensland to Wilson's Promontory in Victoria.

The last 2 million years have seen cycles of climatic change where the world has cooled and then warmed. Evidence of glaciation can be seen in the Snowy Mountains and the highlands of Tasmania – beautiful Lake St Clair is just one stunning legacy of the ice ages. When the ice retreated, the sea level rose, flooding the area we know today as the Bass Strait and cutting Tasmania off from the mainland. Many of the coastal river valleys on the east coast were also inundated and magnificent estuaries like Broken Bay, just north of Sydney, were formed.

Above: Kings Canyon with its spectacular rock formations is an oasis in the Red Centre.

Bottom right: The magnificent corals of the Great Barrier Reef stretch for over 2000km.

Left: Balancing Rock at Glenn Innes, New South Wales, has been sculpted by wind and rain.

Also over this period the great inland sea began to retreat slowly, rivers ceased to flow and the land gradually became more arid. It was during this time that large colonies of coral reefs began to form in the warm waters of the continental shelf off the coast of north-eastern Queensland.

Over the millennia sun, wind and water have carved and hewn the landscape with great artistry – grinding it down into massive sand dunes like Big Red in the Western Desert, cleaving mighty rifts such as Katherine Gorge in the Northern Territory, and smoothing ancient rock formations like the Devils Marbles.

A People and their Land

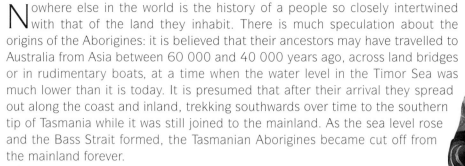

Nowhere else in the world is the history of a people so closely intertwined with that of the land they inhabit. There is much speculation about the origins of the Aborigines: it is believed that their ancestors may have travelled to Australia from Asia between 60 000 and 40 000 years ago, across land bridges or in rudimentary boats, at a time when the water level in the Timor Sea was much lower than it is today. It is presumed that after their arrival they spread out along the coast and inland, trekking southwards over time to the southern tip of Tasmania while it was still joined to the mainland. As the sea level rose and the Bass Strait formed, the Tasmanian Aborigines became cut off from the mainland forever.

When Captain James Cook took possession of Australia for the British in 1770, it is estimated that there were about 300 000 Aborigines living on the continent. Divided into roughly 500 clan groups, they lived both in the fertile coastal valleys and in the vast arid areas of the outback. As hunter-gatherers the Aborigines led a nomadic life, the extent of their travels dependent on the abundance of their food supply, the seasons and their traditions. Since those living near the coast had ready access to water and seafood, they sometimes remained for months in one place, as evidenced by the shell middens they left behind. In the mountains, where food was less plentiful, they had to travel longer distances to gather enough to eat, while in the dry regions of inland Australia where water and food were scarce, Aborigines covered large distances to keep themselves alive. Their knowledge of the availability of food and water resources meant that they had no need to grow crops or domesticate animals. It took only a few hours each day for them to hunt or gather all the food and materials they needed. The seasons also had

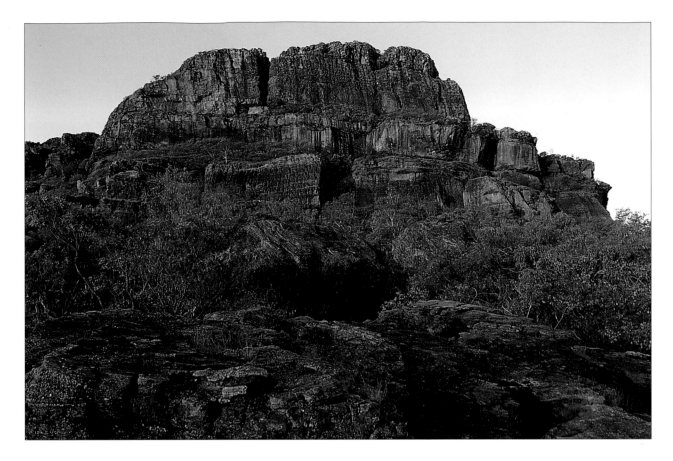

a strong influence on their travels. Often several clan groups would gather in one place to take advantage of migrating animals or fruiting plants. It was at these gatherings that community affairs were discussed, marriages arranged and disputes settled.

The culture and beliefs of the Aboriginal people are strongly bound to the land, plants, birds and animals. The development of this close relationship was not just an issue of survival – the landscape has also played a fundamental part in their spiritual well-being.

Aborigines believe in a time when spirit beings roamed the earth and formed the physical landscape around them. Special sites have particular meanings and their formation and significance are woven into the Dreamtime stories – the myths and legends that have been handed down from generation to generation.

Rising out of a wide, sandy flood plain to a height of 348m, Uluru is one of the world's greatest monoliths. According to

Above: *Imposing and mysterious, Nourlangie Rock in Kakadu National Park contains a wealth of archaeological and rock-art sites.*

Right: *No one knows the age of the Nourlangie Rock paintings, but local Aborigines say they depict the spirit people of the Dreamtime.*

Opposite bottom: *Shaped by the desert winds, this ghost gum near Alice Springs, Northern Territory, reaches into a piercing blue sky.*

the Loritdja and Pitjantjatjara people of the Western Desert, Uluru was created during the Dreamtime. During the course of the day the sun's rays change the colours of the rock, making it easy to understand why this is a place of such spiritual importance for the Aborigines.

Right: Aboriginal X-ray paintings at Kakadu's Nourlangie Rock display a remarkable amount of anatomical detail.

Below: The sacred Memorial to the Dead stands at beautiful Mindil Beach in Darwin.

The springs and caverns at the rock's base are revered as places marking the intersections of invisible paths made by ancestral spirit beings on their wanderings across the land in search of food and water. The prehistoric cave paintings and carvings are also believed to have been made by these beings. The Aborigines tell the tale of Linga, the lizard-man, whose frantic digging for a treasured boomerang created the deep holes and chasms we see today. It is said that Linga took many days to carve his boomerang and when he came to test its flight, it soared across the desert before burying itself in the great red sandhill that was to become Uluru.

More evidence for the existence of these spirit beings is seen at Nourlangie Rock in Kakadu National Park. The local Aborigines believe that the drawings of stick-like figures are self-portraits made by the Mimi – spirit people who still exist today. The Mimi hunt, fish, cook and socialise, just like the Aborigines, but because they are extremely shy, no one ever sees them. When they hear someone coming, the Mimi simply breathe upon the rock which opens before them so that they can slip inside; the rock then closes behind them.

Many natural landforms have a Dreamtime story attached to them. For example, the Devils Marbles which lie 104km south of Tennant Creek in the Northern Territory are a group of granite boulders, some of which are almost perfectly round. The Aborigines believe that these are eggs laid by the Rainbow Serpent. Rock art in the Kimberley, Western Australia, is said to have been made by the Wandjina spirit people who lived during the Dreamtime. Legend has it that if the local Aborigines retouch the art every year, then the Wandjina will ensure their food and water supply.

Every rock and cave, river and tree has some spiritual significance to the Aborigines – a red-coloured rock is the blood of a great warrior, a river the home of the Rainbow Serpent. Their whole environment is imbued with magic and wonder. Because of their special relationship with the landscape, the Aboriginal people are instinctively great conservationists, knowing

just how much they can exploit the earth without upsetting the balance of nature. They have lived in harmony with the landscape that has been their spiritual mother for thousands of years, following a completely sustainable existence.

After the arrival of the First Fleet in 1788, the Aboriginal population declined dramatically through introduced diseases, eviction from their lands and murder by the new colonists. Today, although many Aborigines live in urban areas, some Aboriginal clan groups successfully combine modern and traditional lifestyles in outback communities. As Australians begin to appreciate the significance and strength of the link between Aboriginal culture and the land, attempts are being made by the government to redress the injustices of the past through the recognition of Aboriginal land rights.

Above: *Painted with white clay and ochre, Aborigines perform ritual dances which tell stories of the Dreamtime.*

Below: *According to Aboriginal legend, the Devils Marbles are eggs laid by the Rainbow Serpent in the Dreamtime.*

Left: Lush rainforest edges the scenic drive from Gordonvale up to the Atherton Tableland in Queensland.

European Influences

Unlike the Aborigines, the first Europeans to settle on the Australian continent were at the mercy of the land. The penal colony established in 1788 by the British was hardly an auspicious start to what is now a modern, egalitarian and culturally vibrant country. When Captain Arthur Phillip unloaded his human cargo in 1788, he faced the daunting task of establishing a settlement and supporting his charges in a land where everything was unfamiliar – the birds, trees, animals and plants were unlike anything he had ever seen. Over the next two years, until the Second Fleet arrived, the convicts and officers endured isolation, starvation and misery in a forbidding landscape that had been paradise to the Aborigines they would try to displace.

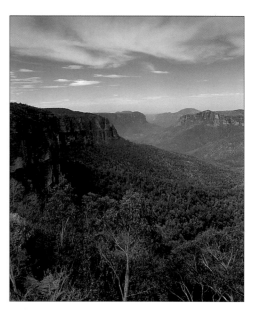

Between 1788 and the early 1800s the European population grew to about 15 000, most of it settling in the Sydney area, although some farmers pushed out into the Hawkesbury Valley to till its fertile soils. As the colony expanded, there was a shortage of good farming land and a need to open up more of the country, but the imposing Blue Mountains presented a seemingly impenetrable barrier to the west. It was only in 1813, when Gregory Blaxland, William Lawson and WC Wentworth set out to find a way across the mountains that the settlers were to discover what lay beyond. With the aid of convict servants, dogs and horses, the three men forged a path up the escarpment through dense bush, along the narrow sandstone ridges that lead westward to the fertile plains beyond what is now the Blue Mountains National Park.

Above: Conquering the sandstone cliffs of the Blue Mountains, New South Wales, seemed impossible to the early European settlers.

During the early 19th century many expeditions were instigated by pastoralists in search of rich grazing lands to sustain the growing colony. Later, expeditions were initiated to search for inland river systems, a possible inland sea and routes across the continent. Many of these were doomed to failure, with both men and equipment ill-prepared for the rigours of journeying through the harsh, arid Australian outback. Explorers lost their lives as they tried to cope with the extreme conditions. Robert O'Hara Burke and William Wills, for example, in their attempt to cross the continent from

Below: The purple night sky at Dalby in Queensland changes these silos into a work of art.

south to north, became separated from their main party. Shunning the assistance of local Aborigines, they died of hunger and thirst on their return from the Gulf of Carpentaria.

The pattern of settlement over the past 200 years has been determined by the Australian landscape, just as the landscape, seasons and climate dictated the lifestyle of the Aborigines. The existence of natural harbours, reliable river systems, arable land and a favourable climate have influenced where Australians have chosen to put down their roots. Today, Australia's fortunes are still largely governed by the landscape and its climate – gentle rain can mean a bumper wheat and wool crop, too much rain brings devastating floods, none at all causes farmers to be driven from the land. These days, many farmers are learning what the Aborigines have always known – working with the land instead of against it brings rewards as the land flourishes and the extremes of climate soften.

Much of the country's landscape has been declared national parkland and several Australian natural wonders have been recognised as World Heritage sites, including the wilderness areas of Tasmania, Kakadu National Park, the Lord Howe Island Group and the Great Barrier Reef.

Australia is a rich country with a diversity of landscapes of every hue. Soft pastel colours of early dawn reflect on the waves as they break on a silver beach; bold ochre and red, maroon and grey-green streak the landscape as the midday sun beats down on the bush; a blazing fireball shimmers as the setting sun turns the sky from shades of apricot to indigo... these are the colours of Australia, the moods of its landscapes changing with the day, the weather and the season.

Above: *A patchwork of vineyards in the Barossa Valley, South Australia's wine region.*

Above right: *Dairy cattle graze the pastures surrounding Berry in New South Wales.*

Right: *Sculpted by long-extinct volcanoes, the Glasshouse Mountains rise regally from rich agricultural plains.*

Outback, Desert and Rock

Above: *The Sturt Stony Desert of north-east South Australia has a stark, almost alien beauty. It was named after the 19th-century explorer Charles Sturt who described it as 'that iron region', where sandhills stand like cliffs above a sea of ironstone 'gibbers' – small round pebbles the colour of blood.*

Opposite top: *To the Aborigines of the Western Desert, Uluru is their most sacred site – it was once inhabited by the spirit people of the Dreamtime. Standing before this massive monolith with its caverns, crevices and waterholes, it is easy to understand its mystical power.*

Left: *The massive rocks of Katatjuta rise from the desert 50km west of Uluru. Steeped in Aboriginal legend, Katatjuta is most spectacular in the evening when the sun's rays paint the rock blood-red, while the purple haze of evening forms a perfect backdrop.*

Above: *Perfectly aligned to magnetic north, these termite mounds are scattered across the landscape of outback Queensland. The reason for this north–south axis is that the termites construct their nests using solar principles in order to present as little surface area as possible to the fierce midday sun.*

Right: *The fearsome-looking thorny devil is really quite harmless. This dragon lizard is covered with dinosaur-like scales which, surprisingly, are neither hard nor sharp. It lives in the arid regions of the western half of Australia, feeding solely on a diet of ants.*

Opposite: *Standley Chasm, near Alice Springs, is a deep cleft carved through the MacDonnell Ranges by an intermittent river which only runs during torrential rain. Bathed in shadow most of the day, the canyon blazes with light when the midday sun turns the rocks flame-red.*

Above: *There is a powerful simplicity in the beauty of the Simpson Desert in South Australia. Spectacular red sand dunes stretch for endless kilometres and crusted salt lakes bake in the sun – dry, silent and waiting. When the rains come, the desert blooms with wildflowers and the waters teem with birdlife.*

Opposite: *The boab tree of Western Australia is only found in the Kimberley. Related to similar species in Africa and Madagascar, its bulbous trunk can reach up to 20m in girth. During the dry season its branches are bare, but when the rains come it blooms with large white flowers.*

Overleaf: *Glowing red in the evening light, these magnificent bluffs and cliffs rising from a sand plain form part of the James Range in the Rainbow Valley Nature Park, Northern Territory. A rainbow effect is created by the bands of iron-red and bleached-white rocks found throughout the range.*

Above: *Tailings from the opal mines of Coober Pedy in the heart of South Australia's outback resemble pyramids in a lunar landscape. Coober Pedy, which is Aboriginal for 'white fella's burrow', experiences such high temperatures that much of the township has been built underground.*

Left: *Shaped like old-fashioned beehives, these domed mountains dominate the Purnululu (Bungle Bungle) National Park in Western Australia. Shrouded in Aboriginal myths and legends, these ancient striped rock formations are dissected by deep gorges with shady waterholes and towering palms.*

Opposite top: *As its name suggests, Wave Rock, near Hyden in Western Australia, looks just like surf about to break on the sand. This unusual 15m-high rock formation is part of an isolated granite hill; its wave-like shape has been eroded over 3000 million years by wind and water.*

Left: *White ghost gums cover the landscape of the Millstream–Chichester National Park in the Pilbara region of Western Australia, where the clay tablelands and basalt ranges are a haven for bird and animal life. As the sun sets the air is filled with bird calls and the buzz of insects.*

Below: *Grassy tussocks, spinifex and white snappy gums march across the upland areas of Millstream–Chichester National Park. Here you'll find cockatoos sitting in coolibah trees, wallabies lazing in the shade below, geckos sunning themselves on the red earth, the air still under an azure sky.*

Bush and Rainforest

Above: Butterflies, like scraps of coloured silk, fly through the lush rainforest near Mount Tamborine in Queensland. Inside the forest the silence is broken only by the call of birds and the pattering of waterfalls and streams which wind past moss-covered rocks, palms and lofty gums.

Opposite top: Clear, fresh water flows over ancient rocks as the Oliver Creek makes its way through the Daintree National Park in Queensland, an area of mountainous country, luxuriant rainforest, majestic waterfalls and abundant birdlife. A place of peace and tranquillity, Oliver Creek is a popular spot for photographers.

Opposite bottom: Dense tropical vegetation crowds the banks of the Daintree's Mossman Gorge. The huge rounded boulders, strewn in the path of the river, are testament to its raging power during the torrential rains of the wet season which sweep the Queensland coast each summer.

Above: The Carnarvon Gorge, north-west of Brisbane, is a spectacular chasm of soft sandstone with almost vertical cliffs. Below lies a forest of stately eucalypts, she-oaks, tall cabbage palms and tree ferns. Only dappled sunlight reaches the many twisting walking tracks that lead through this breathtakingly beautiful national park.

Right: Like layered Japanese fans, these palm fronds form a graphic still-life fit for Gauguin's brush. The inspiration of many an artist, they are typical of the shapes, colours and textures of the plants which form the tangled beauty of the rainforest in the Daintree National Park.

Opposite: A river turns to molten silver in the late afternoon light, while eucalypts jostle for space on the crowded banks waiting for the rains to fall from the clouds gathering in the mountains above. This is the Daintree in all its tropical glory.

Above: The road to Augusta, Western Australia, winds through beautiful karri forests. These tall, elegant trees only grow in a small area in the south-west of the state which receives reliable rain. Rising from a carpet of lush ferns and small flowering plants, they have a quiet, stately beauty.

Left: Mountain ash grow side by side with towering tree ferns in the Tarra–Bulga National Park in the Strzelecki Ranges of south-east Victoria. It is an area of great natural beauty, with inviting walking tracks which make their way under the vaulted canopy of leaves.

Opposite: Magnificent tree ferns, giant myrtle beech and blackwood combine to make Hopetoun Falls one of the most beautiful spots in Victoria's Otway Ranges. In the evening, birds and animals can be seen taking advantage of the pure, clear water as it flows through this pristine gully.

Previous pages: The late afternoon light glows as the sun goes down on the Lamington National Park just outside Brisbane. The park's cool rainforest is rich in flora and fauna, and a walk along its extensive network of tracks will reveal colourful birds and butterflies, splendid elkhorn ferns, orchids and spectacular views.

Above: *The magnificent forests of western Tasmania are truly wild. With raging rivers and unpredictable weather, the region is one of the last unspoilt wilderness areas of the world, containing some of the tallest and oldest living trees, unique wildlife, and rare and endangered birds.*

Below: *As a symbol of Australia, the koala is as instantly recognisable as the kangaroo. This koala lives in the Lone Pine Sanctuary on the Brisbane River, one of the world's largest koala sanctuaries.*

Opposite top: *In the Dorrigo National Park sunshine streams through water droplets into a cave below as if from a crystal chandelier, hence the name, Crystal Falls.*

Opposite bottom left: *The tangled roots of a strangler fig standing beside a boardwalk at Central Station on Fraser Island, off the Queensland coast, reach greedily for the soil.*

Opposite bottom right: *Birds abound in the rainforest canopy of Fraser Island, which is famous for its wide range of flora and fauna, long stretches of golden sand and clear freshwater lakes.*

Beaches and the Coastline

Above: *Pounding waves and winds from the Southern Ocean have taken huge bites from the limestone cliffs of what is known as Victoria's 'Shipwreck Coast', leaving dramatic pillars, chasms, arches and blowholes such as the famous Twelve Apostles and Loch Ard Gorge.*

Opposite top: *Rugged sandstone headlands cradle the golden sands of Garie beach, while crashing surf pounds its foreshores. Situated about an hour's drive south of Sydney in the Royal National Park, the first national park proclaimed in Australia, Garie is popular with surfers, fishermen and families alike.*

Left: *Trawlers lie moored at the Eden fishing wharf. The outstanding natural harbour of Twofold Bay in southern New South Wales was the perfect site for a whaling town which grew into present-day Eden. The area is renowned for its abundant fish as well as for dolphins and the occasional migrating whale.*

Above: *These spectacular blowholes, north of Carnarvon in Western Australia, are an amazing natural phenomenon. As waves crash onto the shore, a powerful jet of water shoots into the air, at times to a height of 20m, creating a sparkling rainbow as it falls to the rocks below.*

Right: *Tessellated pavement (rock eroded into great tile-like segments) is a feature of Eaglehawk Neck which lies on an isthmus joining the Forestier and Tasman peninsulas in Tasmania. In convict days, dogs guarded this narrow neck of land to stop convicts escaping from the penal colony of Port Arthur.*

Opposite: *Not far from Eaglehawk Neck on the Tasman Peninsula is the Devils Kitchen – a vast chasm in the cliff below where the sea boils and churns in a seemingly relentless struggle to demolish the rock. The view from the lookout over Waterfall Bay is spectacular.*

Above: Evening descends on the wharves as the sun sets over the tranquil waters of Lakes Entrance, Victoria, an area renowned as a fisherman's paradise. Not only is it home to the largest commercial fishing fleet in Australia, its lakes and rivers teem with fish for the recreational fisherman.

Opposite: The Twelve Apostles, as seen from the Great Ocean Road in southern Victoria, are massive limestone columns that have been hewn from the land by the relentless action of the Southern Ocean. They are one of many spectacular rock formations to be seen along this coastline.

Previous pages: Sunset paints the evening sky with pinks and purples as light fades over the beach at Tumby Bay on the Eyre Peninsula. Tumby Bay, overlooking the Spencer Gulf in South Australia, is famous for its sheltered waters, white sand beaches, fishing, and safe swimming.

Above: Blenheim Beach forms part of Jervis Bay in New South Wales. The bay is an ecological wonderland of blue waters, white sand, natural bushland and craggy sandstone formations. It is home to bottlenose dolphins and provides a resting place for whales during their migration along the coast.

Below: Australian sea lions are the country's most endangered marine mammal. At the only permanent mainland colony at Point Labatt in South Australia, they can be seen basking in the sun, lazing on the sand, duelling for mates or simply riding the waves in search of fish.

Opposite: Sleepy Bay in Tasmania's Freycinet National Park has a tranquil, serene atmosphere, with small coves and quiet beaches protected by rocky headlands and natural bush.

44

Lakes, Rivers and Wetlands

Above: Elegant river gums reach out over the swollen waters of Cooper Creek at the Cullyamurra Waterhole near Innamincka in outback South Australia. This picturesque area was a favourite fishing spot for Aborigines and provided life-saving water for drovers on their long journey from Queensland to Adelaide.

Opposite top: Palm Valley, west of Alice Springs, seems forgotten by time. Set in a stark landscape, this tranquil oasis is studded with waterholes surrounded by unique, ancient-looking vegetation such as cycads and Livistona palms, which are said to be over 5000 years old.

Left: Beautiful Lake Argyle in the Kimberley is the largest man-made lake in Australia. Studded with many islands that were once hilltops overlooking peaceful valleys, it is ringed with craggy slopes that are now home to indigenous wildlife such as the brush-tailed wallaby and bungarra lizard.

Above: Part of the Territory Wildlife Park near Darwin, Goose Lagoon is a natural waterway where visitors can watch jabiru, pelicans, egrets, geese, and swans from specially constructed hides.

Top: Ubirr Rock overlooks the flood plains of the East Alligator River in Kakadu National Park, Northern Territory. Aboriginal rock art in this area dates back 20 000 years.

Right: Water lilies are found in most still or very slow-moving waters across tropical Australia. Their broad, floating leaves create stepping stones for wading birds.

Opposite: In the parched dryness of the Red Centre lies the cool, verdant Palm Valley. Its clear waters have nourished plants and animals for thousands of years.

Previous pages: Gum trees stand like wooden sculptures against an azure sky at Blanchetown, one of six South Australian locks on the Murray River. Flooded by the saline waters of the Murray, these trees have died back, their bare branches forming perches for passing cockatoos.

Opposite: As you watch the torrent of water plunge to the rocks below, it is hard to believe that the pool below is so calm. Dangar Falls near Dorrigo, New South Wales are one of the most beautiful in a region known for its magnificent mountain, river and bushland scenery.

Below: The evening sky is mirrored in the smooth waters of Tasmania's Gordon River as it glides slowly past Butler Island. While shadows fall, the rocky banks catch the last of the sun's rays, and peace and tranquillity descend on the river.

Above: *The sweeping Gordon dam wall holds back the cold, dark water of Lake Pedder in Tasmania's Southwest National Park. Ringed by spectacular mountains, Lake Pedder has a haunting beauty.*

Opposite top left: *Lake MacLeod is a vast salt lake near Carnarvon in Western Australia. The normally dry lake bed is ringed with ponds constantly being refilled by sea water welling up from caverns below.*

Opposite top right: *The Pioneer River glows red as the sun sets over Mackay in tropical Queensland. The river is the life-blood of the sugar industry centring on the town.*

Opposite bottom: *Clouds hang over the tranquil waters of Lake St Clair in the highlands of Tasmania. Over 200m deep, the lake was gouged from the rock by glaciers during the last ice age.*

Above: *The Tolmer Falls are one of four spectacular water-falls in the Litchfield National Park, south of Darwin. The gorge into which they plunge is so deep that sunlight rarely reaches the valley floor. Unlike other waterfalls which dry up in winter, the Tolmer Falls flow all year round.*

Right: *The Manning River flows peacefully through fertile farming country at Wingham, near Taree in New South Wales. Here, agriculture exists side by side with some of the last pockets of subtropical flood-plain rainforest remaining in the state.*

Mountains, Valleys and Plains

Above: The afternoon light gilds the Three Sisters, a giant rock formation towering over the Jamison Valley, at Katoomba, New South Wales. These famous rocks change colour throughout the day, from red at dawn and dusk to pale yellow at midday.

Opposite top: Golden light spills onto silent fields as the sun rises over Gloucester, New South Wales. The Manning River flows through the area and is joined by three smaller tributaries, the upper reaches of which harbour large numbers of trout.

Left: The Gammon Ranges National Park in South Australia is rugged wilderness country with deep gorges and jagged peaks. In sunlight, the hills sparkle with exposed quartz rock and iron ore. The area is home to the red kangaroo, grey euro and yellow-footed rock wallaby.

Above: *Between mountain ranges and the sea lie the fertile farmlands of Berry in New South Wales. Surrounded by rolling dairy pastures, the town has an English feel with its old deciduous trees and sandstone houses.*

Left: *Flat as a board, these extensive farmlands have been established on the black alluvial soils of Kununurra in the Kimberley, Western Australia. Fed by the irrigation waters from the Ord River Dam, farmers using highly mechanised equipment grow a range of tropical crops for both the Australian and overseas markets.*

Opposite: *Wheat dances in the Western Australian sunlight, the heads heavy with ripening seed. In the distance, the misty foothills of the Stirling Ranges rise above the vast, fertile plains, where sandalwood forests once grew.*

Above: Lush, verdant fields under a summer sky hold the promise of an abundant harvest. Four Pines Farm lies on the fertile flood plain of the Manning River at Wingham, New South Wales.

Below: Eastern grey kangaroos are a common sight in the bushland of the coastal regions of New South Wales. They usually come down to the beach each evening to graze and play.

Opposite: The crystal-clear waters of a highland lake reflect Mount Oakleigh, a craggy range rising like castle ramparts in Tasmania's Cradle Mountain–Lake St Clair National Park.

Previous pages: Mist creeps into the valleys as evening shadows fall over the city of Hobart, seen here from Mount Wellington to its west.

Above: A lone gum tree stands with its mantle of snow. The stark winter beauty of the Victorian Alps is only surpassed in spring when these native grasslands turn into a carpet of colourful wildflowers.

Top: Cradle Mountain rises above Lake Dove in Tasmania's rugged highlands; it is best seen from the Overland Track which winds through forests of deciduous trees, native pines and Tasmanian myrtle.

Left: Lichen-covered rocks, buttongrass and alpine heath give way to woodland and temperate rainforest below snow-covered mountain peaks. These highland meadows below Mount Rufus, in the Cradle Mountain–Lake St Clair National Park, are wild and beautiful.

Above: Water cascades over sandstone rocks as the mountain stream plummets to the Jamison Valley floor. Ringed by temperate rainforest abounding with bird and animal life, Wentworth Falls in the Blue Mountains are named after the explorer William Charles Wentworth.

Right: Ground and shifted into stacks by the glaciers which once covered the area, these huge boulders are a feature of Kosciusko National Park in the Snowy Mountains, New South Wales. These rocks glow at sunrise and sunset and their remarkable shapes resemble flames in a fire.

Opposite: Carved by nature into domes and spires, it's easy to understand why this rock formation was called 'the Cathedral' by early settlers. Standing in Victoria's Mount Buffalo National Park, both its shape and presence echo the ambience of a great European church.

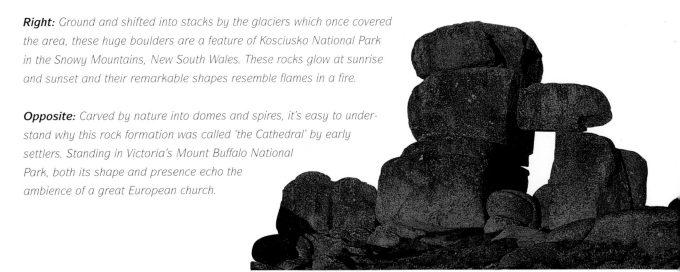

Islands and Reefs

Above: Hamilton Island is a tourist mecca in the tropical waters of the Great Barrier Reef. Part of the Whitsunday island chain, Hamilton is a remnant of a coastal range drowned by rising sea levels at the end of the last ice age.

Opposite top: The sea turns aquamarine as it washes over white sand into a cove at Waddy Point on Fraser Island off the Queensland coast. The world's largest sand island, Fraser has an incredible range of flora and fauna, freshwater lakes and sparkling creeks. Whales can often be seen offshore and green turtles come here to breed.

Left: As the sun sets over Hamilton Island, the evening sky blazes with colour and the blue waters of the Whitsunday Passage turn molten red. By day, cobalt-blue skies hang over dark green islands with pristine sandy beaches.

Above: *The great sweep of Marloo Bay on Fraser Island runs for over 30km from Sandy Cape in the north to Orchid Beach in the south. Although it is the main surfing beach on the island, it is so extensive that peace and solitude can be found by all who seek it.*

Opposite: *Pleasure craft, waiting for the return of scuba divers below, bob at anchor in this peaceful bay on Queensland's Hamilton Island. A drawcard for divers, the island is renowned for its tropical fish and corals, as well as its lush rainforest, seen here crowding the shoreline.*

Overleaf: *Coral beds exposed at low tide reveal the marine life near the beautiful, uninhabited Lady Musgrave Island. Set in the warm, tropical waters of the Great Barrier Reef, this coral cay has an underwater observatory allowing visitors to enjoy the reef's glory.*

Above: *A seaplane flight gives visitors to the Great Barrier Reef a bird's-eye view of the cays. Shoals of fish can be seen from the air as they dart here and there in search of food.*

Right: *The exquisite shapes, colours and patterns of the racoon butterflyfish are typical of the marine life seen on the Great Barrier Reef. The waters of this spectacular living structure are popular with divers and snorkellers from all over the world.*

Opposite top: *The Great Barrier Reef is classified as a World Heritage area because of its biological and geographical complexity. Comprising over 2900 separate reefs it is the richest marine habitat on earth.*

Opposite bottom: *White sands and clear water make Phillip Island an ideal habitat for sea birds and other marine life. After a day spent feeding out at sea, fairy penguins waddle up the beach at sunset, heading for their burrows in the dunes.*

Above: The Southern Ocean pounds the cliffs at Cape du Couedic on the south-west tip of Kangaroo Island, carving great holes through solid rock. Here, colonies of fur seals can be found basking in the sun, and the occasional leopard seal is seen hunting through the surf.

Below: Hewn by icy blasts from Antarctica, the giant Remarkable Rocks look out to sea from the Flinders Chase National Park, Kangaroo Island, South Australia. In the evening light the sun's rays turn these granite boulders russet red.

Opposite: When Commodore Willem de Vlamingh landed on Rottnest Island in 1696, he declared it a 'terrestrial paradise'. Most visitors to the Western Australian island would agree. Here, turquoise waters meet the headland near Bathurst Lighthouse.

Acknowledgements

Above: *The Eyre Highway stretches for endless kilometres through the Nullarbor Plain.*

First published in 1997 by
New Holland (Publishers) Ltd
London • Cape Town • Sydney • Singapore

3/2 Aquatic Drive
Frenchs Forest, NSW 2086
Australia

24 Nutford Place
London W1H 6DQ
United Kingdom

80 McKenzie Street
Cape Town 8001
South Africa

ISBN 1 86436 277 4

Writer: Margaret Gore
Publishing manager: Mariëlle Renssen
Commissioning managers: Averill Chase, Sally Bird
Designer: Laurence Lemmon-Warde
Editors: Jacquie Brown, Anouska Good
Picture researcher: Vicki Hastrich

Reproduction by cmyk prepress
Printed and bound in Singapore by Tien Wah
Press (Pte) Ltd

Photographic acknowledgements

Copyright © in photographs **NHIL** (Shaen Adey) with the exception of the following:

Stuart Owen Fox: pp8 (top right), 11 (top), 64 (bottom); **Frontline** (Stephen Bennett): p7 (top); **Frontline** (Peter Canty): p47;

Frontline (Pete Dobré): p48; **Frontline** (Gerry Velaitis): pp15, 19, 46 (top); **Danja Köhler**: p77 (bottom); **NHIL**: pp14 (top), 22 (top), 27,

34 (bottom), 54, 69 (top); **NHIL** (Anthony Johnson): pp6 (left), 7 (bottom), 8 (bottom), 10 (left), 14 (bottom), 16 (bottom), 17, 20–21,

26 (top), 34 (top), 38, 56, 70 (bottom), 71, 73, 76 (top), 77 (top); **NHIL** (Nick Rains): pp12 (right), 59; **Joe Shemesh**: pp2 (bottom),

29 (top & bottom), 53, 65, 66; **Paul Sinclair**: pp3, 30–31, 32 (bottom), 33 , 67 (bottom), 68, 69 (bottom).

NHIL = New Holland Image Library